DATE NIGHT

BY

THE BADPOETS

I0693790

ACKNOWLEDGEMENTS

A SPECIAL THANKS TO MY BESTFRIEND

THE LONEWOLF (EDITOR)

"To be alive means nothing
If you are not brave enough to live
And to live means nothing
If you are not brave enough to be alive"

PREFACE

Fools are those who turn blind eye to the poetic experiences of
the life.
Cursed are those that are trapped, unable to live the poetic
experiences of the life.
Blessed are those that always swim through the poetic
experiences of the life.

****

Night-the time when all the love comes to life.
Be it the distant love of the Sun for the Moon or
Be it the romantic love of couples embracing each other or
Be it the unrequited love of the broken hearts…
Love never dies in the night.

Date Night is the doorway to words and lines that expresses
the thoughts, emotions and experiences of a couple on their
very first date night.

A boy and girl who love each other more than themselves,
what poetic experiences do they encounter on their first ever
date night?

DATE NIGHT

THE OCEAN'S POV

THE BADPOETS

DATE NIGHT

THE BADPOETS

DATE NIGHT

My life was a gloomy book
filled with nothing but chapters of melancholy
I flipped through the pages in hope
but the word happiness seemed to be long lost.

Never would I have imagined a plot twist
where I would stand in front of a house
on a carefree summer evening
waiting in love.

She had rewritten my genre to a romantic comedy.

DATE NIGHT

The curls of her silky hair
never were a game of fair
cause she knows
from my body my soul bails
every time she does a pony tail

THE BADPOETS

DATE NIGHT

Nor partly nor halfly
But wholly
Nor momentarily nor occasionally
But ceaselessly
I am in a spellbound
By those eyes of my girl
That resemble the black pearls

DATE NIGHT

"How do I look in my date dress?"
-my girl asked

"Even the moon would be jealous at your radiance
what can a mere mortal like me can do
except to bow in silence,
unable to find the words that are worthy of your elegance"
-I surrendered

THE BADPOETS

DATE NIGHT

I visited the florist
in deliberation
to pick up some flowers
that rhyme
with your beauty

but I came out
empty-handed
as I realized
few flowers couldn't be compared
to a walking garden

THE BADPOETS

Quickly cuddle up
The time's not going to freeze up
Let us ride into the blooming night of poetry
My dear lady

DATE NIGHT

Driving in my 90's car
to the far away ocean shore

Listening to the melody
played by my dear lady

My eyes full of delight
as my soul gaze at the golden twilight
welcoming us into our first date night

THE BADPOETS

DATE NIGHT

THE BADPOETS

DATE NIGHT

There's not a soul in the sight
Only the silence of the night
But I have nothing to fear
As I have my whole world right here

THE BADPOETS

DATE NIGHT

My eyes were glowing like a child
As I watch the radiant lamps of the night
Stretching so far, with a count of infinite

The cool breeze carrying the essence of the night
Drenched in the ocean's bite
Made my soul flight

THE BADPOETS

Who could possibly love the ocean, more than the sky?

Always being there in his darkness
Makes his day bright

DATE NIGHT

Who could possibly love the sky, more than the ocean?

Painting her within him
Every time she looks beautiful

DATE NIGHT

The sky resides in the heart of ocean.

DATE NIGHT

The ocean and the sky
A match made in heaven
Imperfectly perfect to complete each other

THE BADPOETS

DATE NIGHT

Just like my woman
that completes
me and my imperfections

THE BADPOETS

DATE NIGHT

She is the starry sky
That lights up
My ocean of darkness

DATE NIGHT

She said stargazing is a love language

She was gazing at the stars
And I was
Gazing at her

THE BADPOETS

DATE NIGHT

Nevertheless the presence
Of these million stars
My lady shines
Brighter than any of them
In my eyes

THE BADPOETS

She - "why aren't you drinking your wine?"

Me - "This bottle of red wine
Never in its lifetime
Can make me get high
In the way I get from your eyes"

"Do you like my eyes that much!"-she blushed

What could I say my love!

7oceans
And more than 50 seas
Yet I still chose
To drown in those eyes of yours

-I confessed

DATE NIGHT

I desire to bite those rosy lips of yours
So that I never forget
That even the sweet elixir
Won't come close enough
To the taste of that honeyed voice of yours

THE BADPOETS

DATE NIGHT

You tame me
As if I were a wild beast,
With your cuteness

You tame me
As if I were a wild beast,
With your shyness

You tame me
As I were a wild beast,
With your fondness

DATE NIGHT

If the stars were to confront me with a choice
A choice between you and the moon
That would be the last time
My eyes would ever see a moon

THE BADPOETS

DATE NIGHT

Oh! my beauty
You don't have to worry
As you are a fairy
Who could make the moon teary
In jealousy

THE BADPOETS

DATE NIGHT

So, my love
Will you bestow me with the chance
To fight the god
For me to be your man
In every rebirth, in every life
Till the infinity ends

DATE NIGHT

Though death do us apart
Even when our bodies rot
My soul will find its way,
To your heart

THE BADPOETS

DATE NIGHT

THE BADPOETS

DATE NIGHT

SCRIBBLE OR ADD

THE BADPOETS

YOUR OWN POEMS OR WORDS

DATE NIGHT

THE BADPOETS

DATE NIGHT

DATE NIGHT

THE BADPOETS

DATE NIGHT

THE SKY'S
POV

THE BADPOETS

DATE NIGHT

THE BADPOETS

I still remember the day
The day I first met you

I stumbled at the sight of you
As I never in my life seen
Someone with so many colours
Yet appear so plain

Like a butterfly
disguised as a caterpillar

Exploring you
was like a drug for me
The addiction only grew
stronger and stronger

DATE NIGHT

My life is nothing less than perfect
With the smile my man brings up
As soon as he lay his eyes on me

THE BADPOETS

DATE NIGHT

That silent smile of yours
Is a killer for my ailurophile heart

THE BADPOETS

DATE NIGHT

My world comes to halt
And my heart starts to beep
As with me his hair flirts
Whenever he does a hair flip

DATE NIGHT

Oh! The wise
That resides in the skies
Did my man fell from the paradise
Cause the moment I see myself in his eyes
I melt away like a doll made of ice

DATE NIGHT

My man's eyes are so dreamy
That I could see my whole life in them

THE BADPOETS

DATE NIGHT

My eyes always click
Him and his memories
So that when I grow old
And recall this album of life
I know that I have been loved
Every minute of my life

DATE NIGHT

Your voice is so seductive
That every time I play a song
I hear you

THE BADPOETS

DATE NIGHT

Living under the delusions
Of your delicious voice
I became a junkie to music

Your music…your voice

THE BADPOETS

DATE NIGHT

You played a verse
That I never dreamt
In my life
My soul would listen

The song's not perfect
Without both music and lyrics

DATE NIGHT

Sometimes it takes more than oneself
To be perfect

THE BADPOETS

Just like my man
that makes me
feel perfect

The ocean is the only home for the sky.

DATE NIGHT

You, are the only home for me.

THE BADPOETS

DATE NIGHT

As a child I prayed hard
Every night

For my darkness
To be illuminated by light

To the radiant stars sailing
in that dreamy ocean above

but never had I thought
that the moon itself
would come down for me

THE BADPOETS

Your eyes illustrated me
In a way I never knew myself

DATE NIGHT

My face's all red
But not because of the chilliness in the air

My eyes are on tears
But not because I am sad

My heart's pounding so hard
That I am afraid it may burst any second

As I watch
My love
On his knees for me
With a ring of love

DATE NIGHT

I would wage war
With anyone that dares to take away
My man's smile

Be it a mortal
Be it an angel
Or be it even me

THE BADPOETS

DATE NIGHT

The waves are dancing
To the rhythm of my happiness

The stars are shining
To the joy in my eyes

The moon bore witness
To my love
As I enter into a new life
By the end of this night

THE BADPOETS

DATE NIGHT

Darling
Please hold my hand
In this night so grand
I don't want to miss the chance
I want you to make my body dance

In this fantasy
With your legacy
Let me have the ecstasies
As you move my body in elegancy

DATE NIGHT

Till the day the oceans dry up
Till the day the sky falls down

Let's embrace each other
in the warmth of love

DATE NIGHT

THE BADPOETS

DATE NIGHT

THE BADPOETS

My three magical words

Y.O.U

DATE NIGHT

THE BADPOETS

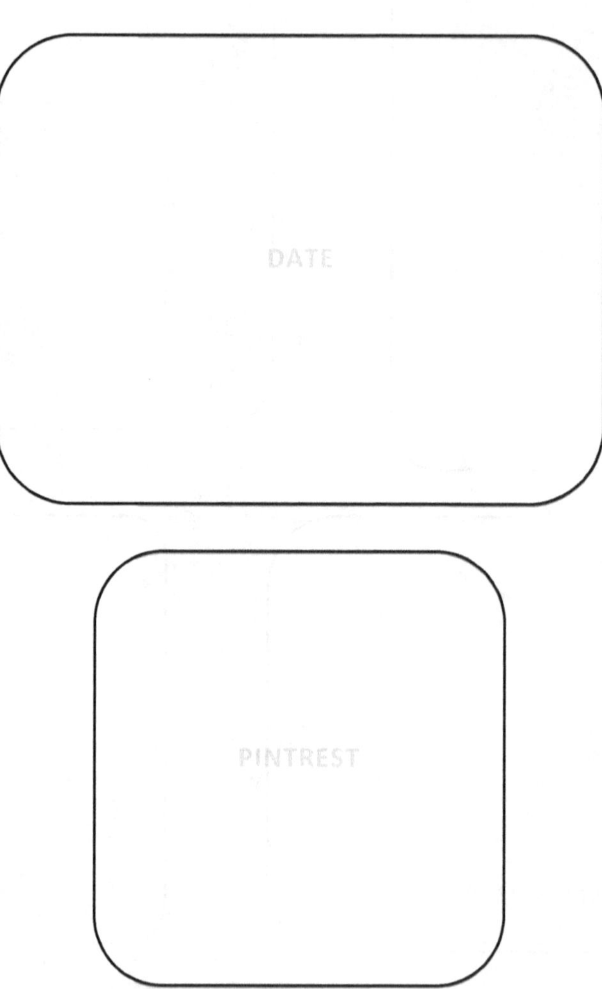

THE BADPOETS

DATE NIGHT

THE BADPOETS

ABOUT THE AUTHOR

***

Hello guys!

I am just your regural average introvert who believes delusion is the only solution. I maybe a bit schizophreniac and my motto is to be at peace one day.

Thankyou guys for reading the Date Night

AND

One more thing, if you never went on a date night this is your sign to experience it and prepare your own DATE NIGHT book with lots of words and pictures so that you can brag about it to your children and grandchildren saying

"In our generation we used to love like this…"

And show them your love…your Date Night book.

THE BADPOETS

www.ingramcontent.com/pod-product-compliance
Lightning Source LLC
Chambersburg PA
CBHW031326250726

48656CB00005B/1990